She Is Me

Also By Vishakha Jain

Sometimes..101 days of healing through words

She Is Me

Vishakha Jain

Disclaimer:

This book is offered as a reflection of personal experiences and perspectives. It is not a substitute for professional help. If you are experiencing emotional distress or mental health challenges, please reach out to a licensed professional or support service. Your well-being matters most.

For more information, contact:

(hello@thespiritualabode.com)

ISBN: 978-1-0694394-2-0

SHE IS ME

"And one day she discovered that she was fierce, and strong, and full of fire, and that not even she could hold herself back because her passion burned brighter than her fears."

- *Mark Anthony*

To maa

*Thank you for being the quiet straw I clung to
when life felt like an ocean I was sinking in.*

VISHAKHA JAIN

Table of Contents

She is Breaking Patterns

She is focusing on releasing the past, healing from pain, trauma, and heartbreak. She is also working on believing in herself more, loving herself for who she is, learning healthy boundaries, and forgiving people *without needing apologies* because she has realized she can't let the past decide who she is, what she is capable of, or all that she can achieve.

She's taking back her power, one step at a time.

She left behind people, places, and situations for a reason — friends, boyfriends, family — whoever they were, they weren't worth draining herself just to fill their cups. Now, she's more mindful about who she allows into her life.

She seeks those who understand the value of *reciprocal love* and *compassion*, those who know when it's time to *stop pouring out* and *start pouring back in*, making sure her cup is also filled when needed.

She kept hearing friends and family asking her why she always overthinks, why she always focuses on the worst-case scenarios. And she wonders how it's so hard for her to explain to them that *being mentally prepared for worst-case scenarios* was the only way she had *survived* so far. *Being hopeful* only to have her hopes and heartbroken is the *worst pain possible,* and she wasn't ready to endure it over and over again, so she did what she had to do to *breathe, keep herself safe,* and *sail through.*

Right people.
Right time.
Until then,
she is *happy* being alone.

Her entire focus is on her *own self* now...
because she realized
she is *worth being the priority*.

The biggest lesson she's learned this year is to *stop forcing things*—conversations, friendships, connections, love, attention. If it's not *flowing naturally*, it's not meant to stay. She's *done begging to be chosen*, *explaining her worth*, or *chasing what keeps running*. What flows, flows. What crashes, crashes. She's *learning to let it*. Because what's *real* won't need to be *forced*.

She says she is done,

but she knows there are 36 more "I am done"

moments

until it's truly over.

And then she wonders why she is the way she is.

She walked away with *scraped knees*,

a broken heart,

and her head held high.

No more getting down on her knees,

begging for *love* that was never hers to keep.

She *loved herself enough* when she walked away from bonds that needed to be *broken* and never looked back. And she *loved herself even more* when she went back and *mended relationships* that were worth *saving*, even when she wasn't at fault.

She walked through the *storm*,
believing it would break her,
but it only washed away
all that was never meant to stay.

Unlearning

She saw the pictures and cried.
The world saw memories.
She saw *flabby arms*, loose skin,
the size she still couldn't accept.

She thought she was past all that
past the *body-shaming*,
past the *dysmorphia*,
past the silent war
with her own reflection.

But one look was all it took,
and suddenly she was back there again,
drowning in old fears, judgment,
the ache of not feeling enough.

That's when it hit her
she still had miles to go,
still had a little girl inside
waiting to be told
that her body was never the problem.

Her only wish?
That someone had told her sooner-
love comes in all shapes and sizes,
and she was never too big
or too small
to be worthy of it.

She was always the one *checking in, holding space,* making sure everyone else around her was okay. But somewhere along the way, she *forgot to ask herself the same.* Now, she's *learning to pause.* To *breathe.*
To ask, *"What do I need today?"* And that one simple question is beginning to *heal years of abandonment,* and the *absence of the love* she needed but never received.

Dear Little Me,

I'm *sorry.*

You went through so much, and no one gave you
the words for it. You thought staying quiet made
you *good.* You thought being helpful would
finally make you *loved.* You thought if you kept
everyone happy, someone would notice when
you were *hurting.*
I know you just wanted to be *held.*
 To be *chosen.* To *matter.* I see you now. I hear
you.
And I'm not going to abandon you the way
others did.
You don't have to *earn* love anymore.
You don't have to *fix everything.*
We're *safe* now. I've got you.

Love,
Me

She's *shedding* the old,
rewriting her life from the inside out,
starting with her *thoughts* and *beliefs*,
then her space,
then her *standards*.

She is in her *soft girl* era.

She texts herself sweet reminders.

Romanticizes slow mornings and hot girl walks.

Buys herself her favorite flowers and iced matcha

lattes. She gives her energy to people who feel

safe.

Spends her time reading books, creating art,

and loving the small inner circle she chose *herself*.

She's not doing it for *attention*.

She's doing it for *peace.*

She is Remembering Her Worth

Sometimes she wonders how it would feel to be *prettier, thinner, curvier,* more *attractive,* more *beautiful.* To be *brown.* Or to be *white.*
All her life, she has only ever looked down on herself, constantly comparing herself, because no one ever taught her that in all her *imperfections* lies her *perfection.* She is *perfectly imperfect,* and that's *beautiful.*

She knows her *value*
and she isn't going to go for
the *bare minimum* anymore.

She deserves someone who sees her,
values her,
and *respects* her.

Heal
and stop letting yourself be
a second choice.
Remember
there is no runner-up trophy
in *love*.

She was never *good enough.*

She never *felt* good enough because she was never taught that she *is* good enough.

It took her *heartbreak* and *hitting rock bottom* to realize that good enough is a *learned behavior.*

Now, she is *healing* and teaching herself that she is *good enough* to be *valued,* good enough to be *seen,*

good enough to be *heard,* and good enough to be *loved* (just the way she is).

She always thought *love was the end-all, be-all*.
Healing made her realize that love *is* indeed the
end-all, be-all, but not the love she was expecting
from Aaron, Danny, or Vishal.
It was the *love she had for herself* all along.

She has reached a point where *success*, to her, means feeling *safe in her home, comfortable in her own skin, confident in her body, loving herself flaws and all*, and being *present enough* to enjoy the little things in life.

She is very protective of her *current self*. It took a lot of *breakdowns*—mental, physical, and emotional—and it took a lot of *spiritual work* for her to reach this stage.

So, if she comes across as if she's *too good* for certain people, situations, events, or conversations,

it's because at this point in her life, she probably *is*.

She knows she is well-read, she works, she
dresses well, she is educated, she is loyal, she has
a *vision*
and *plan* for the future.
She is *healing* and *breaking generational trauma*.
Someone who doesn't *value* that doesn't *deserve*
her.

She lost so much this year—left behind someone she thought she'd never leave, lost friends she believed were her family, and *loved more than she loved herself.*

It's been *tough* and *terribly lonely*, but she had to learn life's biggest lesson: no one is worth loving more than *herself*. She *hopes* that one day she will find her *'right'* people at the *'right'* time.

Until then, she is learning to be *happy being alone*.

She is really into *her* right now. Her *growth*, her *career*, her *self-love*, her *boundaries*, her *health*, her *glow up*, her *mental peace*, and her *happiness*. This time she is *prioritizing herself*!

She realized her love language
is *reciprocity*.
She *deserves* and *needs*
what she gives.
Period.

She never gives up on love until she realizes she's being *ignored*, *taken for granted*, or *manipulated* into feeling *worthless* through gaslighting. And when she finally gives up, she leaves in *silence*. No long paragraphs, no *we need to talk* conversations, no *begging*, no *fighting*, no *justifying*, no *proving*, no desperate attempt to fix a relationship that was already *broken*.

She is Hope and Healing

She
became
the
peace
she
was
seeking
outside.

Sometimes, she feels it's easier to give up than to keep going back and forth with *healing*, constantly challenging her *negative thoughts* and *emotions*. It feels *daunting*, harder than she thought, and at times, it even gets *overwhelming*. But the reality is, her current situation isn't what she was *hoping* and *praying* for. So, every day, she tries, taking *tiny baby steps*, hoping one day it won't be this hard to heal her *mindset* and manifest a *new life*, a *new reality*, and a *happier*, more *confident* woman.

She is *happy* the way she is,
unbothered,
totally content
in her *self-care* era.

Sometimes, she *craves* and *longs* for a life where she has the *love* she desires, all the *money*, the *body*, the *status*—a life that is *rich* and *elite*. But *healing* makes her realize that not every *rich* person is *happy* in love, not every *beautiful* person is *secure* in their body, and not every *elite* sleeps *peacefully* at night. Because it's not about the relationship, money, looks, or social circle; it's about being *valued* and *respected* in a relationship, having *peace* at home, feeling *happy* and *secure* within her body, and finding *contentment* before she closes her eyes every night.

She *fell*,
she *broke*,
she *stumbled*,
she *failed*,
but then
she *rose*,
she *healed*,
she *overcame*,
she came back...
and *how*.

She is quietly *healing,*
dreaming,
and *manifesting.*

The *small gestures*
matter to her
the most.

She is at a point in life where, on some days, she's all revved up and ready to take on the world: making massive amounts of money, starting a side hustle, focusing on her *glow-up*, starting meditation, joining a gym, and doing meal prep. But on other days, she just wants to stay in bed, browse the internet, do a massive amount of online shopping, have someone pay all her bills, and be served breakfast in bed. May she find a way to *rest* and still *achieve* her dreams.

She is at a stage in life where she knows she needs to lose weight to become healthier, but she is *tired* and doesn't want to start from scratch all over again. She has been restricting her diet, counting calories, trying fasting, keto, paleo, and more over and over again ever since she was a *kid*. Now, she's *fed up*, she's *exhausted*. She's focusing on *healing her inner child,* addressing her *fears*, and fixing her relationship with *food*. However, her family, friends, and even she herself have a hard time accepting her the way she is. Hoping that one day either she'll become the version of herself she thinks she has been in love with or end up *falling in love with herself,* weight, stretch marks, loose skin, and all.

Believe in your own *worth,*
because you are worth the *respect,*
worth the *time,*
worth the *effort,*
and worth being the *chosen one.*

She *deserves*. She deserves to be *loved* for who she is, *scars and all*. She deserves *success* for all the hard work she's put in. She deserves *abundance* for all the times she had to *survive* instead of thrive. She deserves *happiness* and *peace* for every moment she felt *broken*, *lost*, and *forgotten*. Yes, she *deserves*. And she deserves *more* than she's ever been taught to ask for.

Hey girl,

Stop with the *constant comparison* and seeking love from outside. Go *within* and give love to that *wounded inner child* who is hiding somewhere inside of you, *longing* and *waiting* for your love and acceptance. Remember, she is just a *child* looking for the day you would come *back home* and hug her.
Go back home, beautiful!

You're entering a *new reality* where everything will start to go your way.

Your *time is coming,* and it's going to be one of the *best times* of your life.

Feel it, believe it, Trust it, manifest it and *claim it!*

If I could go back
and tell her anything,
all I would say is
it wasn't her fault,
he wasn't the one,
but she's *good enough*
and *worthy*
to be *loved by default*.

She thought losing weight would finally make her *happy*, but it didn't. Then she believed that finding the *perfect relationship* and falling in love would fix everything, but most of them brought *heartbreak* and *karmic lessons* she wasn't ready for. After that, she thought being alone would bring her *peace*, but *loneliness* crept in during the quiet moments and made the silence harder to bear. This cycle kept repeating, breaking her a little more each time, until she finally realized the *truth*. *Happiness* wasn't waiting for her to be in a smaller body, someone else's love, or even in solitude. It was something she had to find *within herself*, in every moment, just as she was.

She doesn't know how to feel anymore. One moment, she thinks she's *healing*. The next, she's *questioning everything* about herself. One moment, she's *laughing* like she's finally *free*. The next, she's *holding back tears*, trying to keep from falling apart. She just *hopes* that one day, or maybe someday, it'll all make sense. Until then, she's *healing, stumbling, learning,* and *growing*—one day at a time.

She is Rewriting Her Story

Worthy

She was a *free bird*, lost in her world.
Beautiful, *independent*, and *carefree*,
until a man came along, saw her, wanted her,
and gave her a kind of love she never thought
could be.

The *love*, the *care*, the *attention*, the *dream*
she got swept away, thinking this was her
destiny.
Never-ending conversations, all the texts,
the flowers, the dinners, the long drives,
those long talks ending with the early morning
light.

He was everything she dreamed her prince could
be.
Slowly, she fell in love,
believing it was what was meant to be.

Until her world came crashing down
when he showed up
with a picture of another woman
in a red gown.

"*Fiancée,*" he introduced her.
"*Five years* is how long we've been together."
She wanted to scream, wanted to cry,
had questions deep and wide,
but instead, she blamed herself,
pushed her pain aside.

Guilt, shame, and the feeling of being *not enough*
made her believe she was to blame.
Instead of holding him accountable,
she built her walls *iron-strong*
and vowed never to let another man cause her
pain.

Too many summers, monsoons, and winters
passed by,
and she never allowed another man to come
nearby.

If I could go back and tell her anything,
all I would say is,
it wasn't her fault.
He wasn't the one.
But she's *good enough*, and *worthy*,
to be *loved by default*.

Sometimes, when she looks back on her life, she sees *pain*, *mistakes*, and *heartache*.
But when she looks in the mirror, she sees *strength*, *learned lessons*, and *pride* in herself.

She is
finding herself
all over again.

She's in a *strange place* where her *old self* is gone. But the *new her* is still a *work in progress*. She realizes that *healing, change,* and *growth* are *scary, unknown,* yet *beautiful* all at the same time. She is trying to be *kind to herself* as she is *growing through* what she is *going through*.

She grew up thinking life is *pink* and *glitter* and *unicorns* and *fairy tales*. Only to realize, adulting is all about handling all the *shades of grey*, *fighting* and *slaying demons* both internally and externally, *protecting* her *self-respect*, her *dreams*, her *castle*, and fighting to *survive* and *thrive*.

She believed in love; she was in love with *love*. However, one day, that love left her with *hundreds of unanswered questions* and *broken promises*. Despite numerous attempts to find answers, she failed. Eventually, she realized that through all this *pain, suffering,* and *transformation,* she was meant to *love herself* to *find herself.* That was the only answer she needed *all along.*

She lost herself trying to make everyone around her *happy*. Now she is losing everyone around her while trying to *find herself* again.

She spent years *hoping* and *praying* to find someone who can hold her hand in public, to walk proudly beside her. *Healing* made her realize that the only reason she *needed* and *craved* public displays of affection was to prove to others that she was just as *deserving* of love as anyone else. To show them that *look I found what you all thought I couldn't*.

She is learning to be an entrepreneur, *healing*, and *growing* to build a beautiful legacy. But there are days when she gets *tired* of people questioning her work, questioning her lack of tangible results, and people telling her she is wasting her time. Somewhere, she also starts questioning *herself*. Yet every day, she wakes up fueled by the *belief* that she will prove everyone wrong, that her *resilience* and *strength* will pay off one day, and her *success* would be the ultimate response to all those who doubted her, including *herself*.

She isn't *lost*, she's just at a stage of her life where her *old self is gone*, but her *new self* isn't fully here yet. She is in the *middle* of her massive *transformation* and *glow up*. She is getting all the signs from the universe that *everything is working out in her favor*. She's *next in line for blessings*.

When you tell yourself you're *good* at something, it starts showing up in your life. If you *believe* you're good at sales, you'll attract more sales. When you think you're good at making money, more money comes in. If you *feel happy* in your body now, you'll start seeing the changes you've wanted for so long.

Feel worthy, feel enough and watch the universe conspire to fulfill your dreams.

Today I cried for that little girl in me who had *dreams*. Dream of being *successful* in her 20s, dream of getting *married* with 2 little kids and her own white picket fence in her 30s. Dreams that she had to *crush* one by one because deep down she didn't believe she was *worthy* or *enough*. I wish I had gone back to her sooner to tell her that she is *intelligent, brave, smart, strong* and she is so goddamn *worthy* and *enough*!
She is *unique* and so *beautiful,* and her *time is coming*. Maybe a bit late but *age is just a number,* keep *dreaming* because her life is going to get magical for her!

She often *daydreams*
about rejecting the *apologies*
she knows she may never receive.

She may have lost someone
who didn't *love* her,
but they lost someone
who truly *loved* them
unconditionally.

Some days, she feels like she's *moving forward*.
Other days, she feels like she's *falling apart all over again*. But deep down, she knows healing isn't perfect. It's *messy, unpredictable*, and hers to navigate in her *own time*.
And even in the chaos, she is *stumbling, healing*, and still *growing*.

She remembers *crying in the middle of the night,* clutching her chest as though holding herself together would stop her heart from breaking. But somewhere in the *pain* and *grief,* she began to find pieces of herself she thought she had lost. The woman she's becoming isn't free of scars, but she's *stronger, wiser,* and finally realizing she is *worth showing up for, worth choosing,* and *worth fighting for.*

Life gave her more *lemons* than she could carry.
Everyone said, "Make lemonade." Instead, she
picked up a pen and turned her *pain into poetry*—
words laced with *comfort* and *relatability*, so
someone else could feel a little less *alone* when
their world felt *bitter* too.

She is Craving Something Real

She wants someone who will fall in love with her *messy bun, oversized T-shirt, baggy eyes,* and *tiger stripes.* Someone who finds it *adorable* when she continually bumps into furniture, trips over her own two feet, or forgets why she walked into a room. She wants someone who can make decisions for her when she's *indecisive* about what to eat, who can be her *safe space,* and who will still love her and hold her hand when she's *old and gray,* even if she forgets what day it is—or forgets *everything except his name.*

Sometimes, or rather, most of the time, she isn't looking for *advice*. What she truly needs is a *shoulder to lean on*, a *hand to hold*, an *ear to listen*, someone who makes her feel *seen and heard*, and a *heart that understands* her.

Sometimes, all she desires is to manifest someone with whom she can share things she hasn't told anyone before. She longs for a *safe space* where she can speak about her *scars*, her *broken heart*, the *raw pain*, and her *vulnerabilities* without fear of *rejection*, knowing she'll be met with nothing but pure *love, acceptance, compassion,* and *understanding*.

Sometimes all she *desires* is to manifest someone with whom she can share things she *hasn't told anyone before.* She *longs* for that *safe space* where she can speak about all the *scars*, the *broken heart*, the *raw pain*, the *vulnerabilities* without the fear of *rejection*, knowing she'll be met with nothing but pure *love*, *acceptance*, *compassion*, and *understanding*.

She is *torn* between letting go of her *fears* and breaking down her *walls*, or finding *love* while still *safeguarding* her own *heart*.

She's at a stage where she wants to *lose those extra pounds* but doesn't want to do anything about it. She's *longing for love* but absolutely *loathes* the idea of signing up on dating sites. She wants to be *spiritual* and *connected with nature*, but let's be real, she'd much rather cozy up with another season of Bridgerton.

She's *hoping* that one day, someone will just barge into her house professing their *undying love* for her while she's chilling in her pajamas, doing her 7-step skincare routine, munching on cookies, and Netflixing away.

Right people
right time
until then
happy being alone

She is *scared* of love, *scared* of being in love and being loved by the *wrong person*. What if she lets someone in and he ends up *breaking her heart* again? What if she has to *pick up the pieces* of her heart and *glue them back together* all over again? She is *scared*, *afraid*, and *exhausted*. Because of this fear, she is torn between *learning to be happy alone* or *preparing herself to settle for less* than what she really *deserves*.

She just wants to let her guard down and be *vulnerable* for once, as she is *tired* of always being *strong*. All she *desires* is to feel *safe* and *secure*, but wonders if that's *too much to ask*.

When she tells you about her problems, it doesn't mean she's *complaining*; it simply means she *trusts* you enough to make her feel *seen* and *heard*.

She is *tired* of all the first dates and telling them her favorite color. She just *hopes* to find someone who is both her *safe place* and her *biggest adventure*—a person who *accepts her fully* yet *pushes her to grow* and reach her highest potential. Someone who *fights for love, prioritizes her*, and makes her feel *seen* and *heard* in the same way she does.

She doesn't want a *perfect* relationship because *perfection isn't real*. Instead, she desires a relationship built on *trust, honesty, loyalty, love,* and the *small imperfections* that make it *genuine* and *real*.

She may be plus size, but she is a
human too. She also wants to feel *loved*,
to be *accepted*, to be *cherished* too. Let's
stop *demonizing* weight. Remember,
extra kilos don't diminish someone's
ability to *give* and *receive love*.

She is at a point in her life where she
just wants to *hug someone* and tell them
how *tired* and *drained*, she really is,
someone who can make her feel *safe*,
seen, *secure*, and *protected*.

When was the last time you felt *unconditional love, unconditional acceptance*? Do you crave for *"I love you and accept you just the way you are"* type of love? It could be a strong *yearning* or a tiny hidden *desire* to find *"the one"* who doesn't care about your flaws but rather considers them as *perfect imperfections*. If you do, girl, that's okay! Your *feelings are valid*. But ask yourself, my love, when was the last time you gave *yourself* that *unconditional love and acceptance* that you are seeking from the outside world? It's never too late. Today, make a *promise* to that inner child who is *hurt* and feeling *lost* that you will always be there for her, *loving* and *accepting* her *unconditionally*, just the way she is.

She is Ready for Love

She's at a point where she enjoys being *single*, loving the *freedom* to do things her own way. But inside, she quietly dreams of finding a *love story* that truly fits into her life just right—a love that makes her feel *seen* and *heard*, a *safe space* that allows her to be *vulnerable* for once in her life, as she is *tired* of being strong all the time.

She's eagerly awaiting that one person who will take the time to sit her down, look into her *eyes* and her *soul*, and declare:

"You are perfect just the way you are.

I'm not giving up on you.

You're the one for me.

I'm committed to treating you the way you deserve to be treated.

I'll learn how to love you right, and I'm not going anywhere.

Because for me, it's all about you."

She hopes to find a *love* that makes her feel *giddy* and *happy* like a child—something that helps her forget all about pain, past trauma, and old baggage. A love that *warms* her heart and makes her *glow*. A love in which she wakes up every day feeling *secure* and *appreciated* for who she is, inside and out.

You are *worth keeping,*
worth committing to,
worth making a priority,
and *worth loving.*

It's okay to *want love*; it's okay to seek a *loving,* *caring,* and *safe* relationship. It's absolutely fine to seek *The One*. But don't forget, the most *beautiful* *relationship* is the one you have with yourself. *Love yourself first*, feel *safe* in your own body first, and learn to treat yourself as a *priority*. Only then will you teach others how to *love* you, *treat* you, and *prioritize* you.

She wonders if *love* is blind or if it makes you blind. Love is neither blind nor does it make you blind. Love is, in fact, the *clearest mirror*, reflecting your *deepest fears* and *insecurities*, forcing you to face them whether you're ready or not. Love neither blinds you nor is it blind; it is your *greatest fear*, a *powerful catalyst*, the *ultimate life lesson*, and, at times, a *profound healer*.

She can scream, she can cry, she can let the whole world know why. But what she truly *desires* in the end is someone who *hears her silence*. Because *silence* is the language only two *destined souls* understand.

She's been *searching for love* in all the wrong places, seeking it from all the wrong people. Maybe it's time she asks for *love* from the one person who has been there all along, the one staring back at her in the *mirror*. Maybe that's where she'll find the kind of love she's been *waiting for*, the *in sickness and in health* kind of love, the *no matter what* kind of love, the *love that never leaves*.

Love was supposed to feel like *home*. At least, that's what she was told. But instead, love gave her *trauma*, *gaslighting*, *silent treatments*, *depression*, and *anxiety*.

Now, she's healing from the kind of love that felt like *war*, the kind that made her question her *worth*, her *voice*, her *softness*. She's learning to feel *safe* in her own skin again, to *believe* in her worth, and to *trust* that love doesn't have to *hurt* to be real.

Dear Her,

Stop chasing love that *confuses* you.
If it makes you question your *worth*, it's not love.
Love doesn't make you *beg*.
It doesn't *punish* you with silence.
You deserve better.
Not one day, *now*.

She still *believes* in love.
She just doesn't believe
in *settling* for it anymore.

She's *tired* of being told to move on, to let go, to stop feeling so much. What they don't understand is that her *feelings are valid*, her *pain is real*, and her heart is *healing* in its own time. She doesn't need to be *rushed* or *fixed* she just needs to be *loved* for who she is, right here, right now.

She is Soft and Powerful

She wants to be *vulnerable*
for once in her life
because she is *tired*
of being *strong*.

She took a deep breath,
channeled an *inner strength*
she never knew she possessed,
and whispered to her soul,
I got this.

She's *amazing*; her *strength* is her superpower, not her kryptonite. Her *never-give-up* spirit showcases how *resilient* a strong woman can be. Having been through *hell and back,* she still stands *tall* and *proud*. It took her a while, but she now realizes that she can achieve *anything* she sets her mind to. Don't mess with her; she's *unstoppable* now.

Strong women feel it all
the *anger,*
the *heartbreak,*
the *exhaustion*
but they still choose *love,*
time and time again.

You're the *full story—soft chapters, strong endings,* and all the *underlines in between.* You are the kind of *magic* people only *dream* of meeting. A *dreamer.* An *old soul.* Someone who *feels too deeply.* Too *real* in a world full of filters and edits. She's *not an illusion.* She's *not a fantasy.* She's *real.* She's *you.* And *she is me.*

She believed she could, so she did?

No, she didn't. She was *tired*. She was *exhausted*.

She was *drained*. What she needed was a nap—a

very good nap. A *cozy blanket*, a few candles, some

Chinese takeout, and a little Netflix.

 So, she did exactly that.

Some days healing will look like *routines* and *resilience*. Other days, it will look like *Netflix*, *crying*, and *not answering texts*. Let *both* counts. Let *both* be *holy*. You're doing *better* than you think.

When she finally *believed* in herself, nothing could stop her. Not the *doubt.* Not the *past.* Not even the voice that once told her she wasn't *enough.*

Unseen Battles

She is the kind of woman
who will *cry* in a corner,
collect herself *quietly,*
and walk back into the room
in her *six-inch heels,*
with *steady hands*
and a *soft smile,*
no one ever knowing
the *storm*
she just survived.

She wasn't born
to be *chosen*.
She was born
to *choose*.
#learningthedifference

She didn't ask
to be *saved*
she became the *storm*
and the *shelter*.

She was too *broke* to hire a therapist.

The men in her life gave her more *trauma*

and *trust issues* than advice.

So she made *ChatGPT* her therapist,

her friend,

her 24/7 emotional support system.

She is *resourceful* that way.

She is *me*.

She is *love*.

She is *laughter*.

She is *rare*.

She is *real*.

She is *beautiful*.

She is a *diamond*.

She is *you*.

And she is *me*.

She's been through *hell*,
but she still *smiles*.

She's *soft*,
but don't test her twice.

She's *growth*.
She's *grit*.
She's *glow*.

She is a *force*.
And she is *power*.

One of her worst habits?
She still *cares*
even after they *hurt* her.

When
she
sets
her
mind
even
the
stars
align

She is Freedom and Becoming

She is *living her best life,*
not bothered
about what others think.

She is committing to loving herself *unconditionally*, *healing* past wounds, and *manifesting* her dreams. She promises to *honor* her worth and *nourish* her soul. This coming year, she will focus on chasing her dream of buying designer bags and exploring dream destinations, rather than chasing unavailable men and unrequited love. It's her time to *glow up*, *shine*, and *thrive* in the power of being *herself*.

She is making this year her *quietest* era.
She simply wants to *travel*, work on her *mind* and
body, find ways to *love herself more*, start a *side
hustle*, make *money*, and *enjoy her own company*.
She doesn't want to hear anyone's issues, as she
won't be sharing hers. She has room only for
genuine connections, accepting only *reciprocal love*
that makes her feel *valued*, *loved*, *heard*,
appreciated, and *cherished*.

The day she stopped
obsessively checking
his *last seen* status
was the day
she felt *free*.

Let her love the way she *wants* to love.

Let her be loved the way she *dreams* to be.

Let her grow into who she's *meant* to be.

And if you can't, then let her be by *setting her free*,

so she can become *everything* she was meant to

be.

She held *hope* in one hand,
heartbreak in the other,
and somehow, still…
smiled
with *tears* in her eyes.

She stopped chasing people
who took hours to text back
but watched her *stories* in real time.
She stopped *overexplaining* herself
to those committed to misunderstanding her.
Now she pours that energy
into *herself,*
her *skincare,*
her *side hustle,*
her *mindset*
her *soft mornings,*
and *manifesting the life she always wanted.*

Healing doesn't mean adding another to-do list
or following a structured morning and evening
affirmation and meditation routine.
Healing also comes in… *sleeping in.*
Ignoring texts because she's tired.
Watching the same show for the third time.
Crying for no reason. Not knowing what the hell she's
doing — and still showing up anyway.
It's not always *pretty*. But it still *counts*.

She is *stumbling,*
learning,
healing,
growing
and *glowing.*

She doesn't need another *narcissist*, another *heartbreak*, or another *life lesson* wrapped in *pain*. What she really needs is a few million dollars, an *unlimited supply* of matcha's and iced coffee, the ability to eat whatever she wants and not gain weight, and a *book boyfriend* on a cozy Sunday morning — preferably with dimples,
5 o'clock shadow, *touch her and you die* kind of vibe.

She is going to *win* this year,
and that's the *end* of the story.

She's becoming
who she *needed*
when she was *younger*.

Hey *beautiful* girl,
focus on *improving* yourself,
not constantly *proving* yourself.

She pays for *unlimited calls*.
Talks to *no one*.
She is *me*.

She's in a season of *letting go* of people who
drained her, of memories that *broke* her, and of the
idea that she has to be *everything for everyone.*
She's finally learning to be *enough* for herself.
And that is her greatest *freedom.*

She's in a season of *rediscovery*. She's letting go of the version of herself that felt *small* and *unsure,* and she's stepping into a space where she can finally see her own *worth*. It's *terrifying*, *unfamiliar*, and *beautiful* all at once. But she knows she *deserves* to find herself again, no matter how long it takes.

Do Not Disturb

She turned off *read receipts,*
left a few texts on *delivered,*
muted *stories,*
and started sleeping with her phone on *do not
disturb.*
Not to be petty,
but to protect her *peace.*

She no longer feels *guilty*
for choosing her *peace* over *chaos,*
for *distance* over *disrespect,*
for *emotional regulation*
over *instant gratification.*

She is No Longer Apologizing

She's at a point in her life where she is *happy being alone* and *okay* with people not liking her. She is fine with others not understanding her side of the story and is *least bothered* by what they think. She doesn't owe anyone an *explanation* or an *apology*. She is here to live her life on her *own terms* and by her *own rules*. She is choosing *peace, truth, real authentic love*, and—above all—she is choosing *herself*.

She is at a point in life
where she no longer allows herself
to *suffer for love*.
If you ever see her *sad,*
it's because either her *knee* hurts
or her *stomach* does.

She's reached a point where being *pushed too far* can make her avoid you completely. In any relationship — friends, family, or romantically — *constant negativity* or *stress* can lead her to step away for her *well-being*. Even she has her *limits*; respecting her *boundaries* is crucial for her *mental health* and *peace*.

And one day, she realized that people don't have to *like* her, people don't even have to *love* her, or even *respect* her. But when she looks at herself in the mirror, she better *love* herself, she better *choose* herself, and she better start *respecting* herself. Above all, she better start *standing up* for herself.

At this point, nothing can bring her down because she isn't afraid to eat alone or walk away from relationships, even if it means losing friends.

She isn't afraid of being alone, doesn't care about rejection or heartbreaks, and no longer tolerates *disrespect*. She is finally choosing *self-respect* over drama and *disrespect*.

Let her be the girl
she was *born to be*.
Don't let her turn into
a *shell of herself*
just because you're *indecisive*
about your feelings.

Know your *worth*!
You are not a *wallflower*
available at a *garage sale*.

She once *longed* for a love that would move *heaven and earth* for her. But now, she's *done waiting.*
Instead of expecting this kind of love from others,
she's finally *giving it to herself.*

She Was Meant For More

She wasn't born to *wait around* until she was
picked.
She was *meant to be seen*.

She wasn't born to be compared
to *skinny Instagram models* or *curvy Pinterest pins*.
She was *meant to be cherished* exactly as she is.

She wasn't born to *earn love* through her
performance.
She was *meant to be loved* simply because she
exists.

She wasn't born to *beg for breadcrumbs* of
affection.
She was *meant to be loved*, to be *chosen*,
to be *cherished*, and to be *celebrated* just as she is.

Dear me,

Just because no one told you before doesn't mean it's not true now:

You are allowed to take up space.

You are allowed to want more.

You are allowed to be loud, visible, messy, magical,

you.

Just in case you needed a reminder,

No one taught you this growing up, so I'll say it
now: *You are not too much.*
You are not asking for *too much.*
You're *allowed* to take up space.
You're *allowed* to want real love, soft days, and
more for yourself.

She got *tired*
of waiting to be *chosen,*
so she *picked herself* instead.

Limerence

She wanted to grieve; she wanted to cry.
Her pain ran deep and wide.

But how do you open up about walking away
from something that only ever lived in your
mind?

How do you explain mourning a love
built on maybes, almosts, and what-ifs?

So, she stayed quiet,
carrying a heartbreak no one could see.

But she's done regretting
because in that moment, her love was real.
Her grief was real.
Even if the relationship never was.

She *feels* deeply,
loves wildly,
and walks away quietly.

Some days she is *prayer*.
Some days she is *thunder*.

She is Not the Same Anymore

She's no longer the *same*.

Her heart rests in *calm* instead of *storms*.

That's how she found her way back.

She became her own calm, and she refuses to settle for anything less.

And it's beautiful.

It's *beautiful*.

She changed, but not because she wanted to; she was *forced* to. It wasn't overnight like in the movies you see. Slowly, painfully, over the years—through heartbreaks, through grief, through sleepless nights, through gut-wrenching tears. But eventually, she *did*. Though she has her moments of doubt, now she isn't afraid to walk away from anyone or anything where she isn't *appreciated* and *respected*.

There were moments when she looked in the mirror and didn't recognize herself. She had been carrying so many versions of herself just to make others comfortable that she *forgot* who she truly was at her core. But now, she's reclaiming herself *piece by piece*. She's starting to see her reflection again—and for the first time in a long time, it feels like *home*.

She remembers standing in the rain,
waiting for someone to come back, for someone to
choose her, to *pick* her, to *love* her. But the storm
passed, and she was still standing. That's when
she realized she was *never going to be the same
again*. She wiped her own tears and vowed never
to let anyone make her feel like an *option* again.
That day, she began her journey to becoming the
confident woman she was meant to be, because
the old *doormat* version of her was *washed away*,
just like the memory of a *love that was never hers
to begin with*.

It took her a while to notice that her so-called soulmate liked having her around—not for *love*, but simply out of *habit*. And the hopeless romantic in her called that a *connection*. So, she kept brushing off the weight she was carrying just to keep the conversation going. Told herself it wasn't a big deal. That maybe *this* is what love looks like. But over time, the silence in her grew louder—not out of anger, just *clarity*. And when she finally walked away, it wasn't to prove a point. It was the moment she realized she had *lost herself* just to fit into someone else's free time.

She's not *cold*.
She just doesn't serve *warm* energy
to people who left her in the *dark*

.

They say, *"She changed."*

Well... yeah.

She stopped saying *yes* when she meant *no.*
Stopped shrinking just to be liked.
Stopped fixing what she didn't break.

She's softer now—but with boundaries.
Kinder—but unavailable to drama.

She didn't just *change.*
She *woke up.*

She stopped *breaking* herself for someone who never stayed to *pick up the pieces.*

She doesn't leave with *drama*.
She leaves in *silence*.
Because when she's *done*,
there's *nothing left to explain*.
Her *silence* becomes the answer.

She was all of it.

The *Kali* — in her rage, her endings, her sacred
no.

The *Durga* — in her protection, her softness, her
fight to hold it all together.

She was the *storm* and the *silence* after.

The *boundary* and the *balm*.

The *destroyer* of what hurt her.

The *creator* of what came next.

She's the kind of woman
who notices *everything*.

So, if you think she didn't see it,
she *did*.

She just chose
to stay *quiet*.

If you're constantly criticized,
you better believe,
girl,
you're doing something *right.*

She's at a place in her life where she's *done* trying to prove her worth. She's *tired* of bending and breaking just to fit into spaces that were never meant for her. She's learning to *choose herself,* to let go of people who *drain* her, and to stand firmly in her own *light.* Because the right people will see her *value* without her having to fight for it.

She wasn't waiting to be *loved*;
she was quietly learning to *love herself,*
one small step at a time.

She spent years trying to be everything for everyone, wearing a smile even when her heart was *heavy*. But now, she's learning to say *no* without guilt, to *rest* without shame, and to love herself the way she loves others. She's finally realizing she deserves the same *kindness* she so freely gives.

If you're in a season of healing and growing
through what you're going through,
these pages were written for you.
Because this is my story,
and it's yours too.
She is me. She is you.

Thank you for journeying through these pages with me. I hope these words found a soft place in your heart, just as they did in mine while writing them.

If you feel called to share how this book touched you, I'd be deeply grateful if you leave a review. Your words help others find these pages too.

If you'd like to stay connected or read more, you can find me as @thespiritualabode

Feel free to write to me at

hello@thespiritualabode.com

You can find my work here:

instagram.com/thespiritualabode

facebook.com/thespiritualabode

tiktok.com/thespiritualabode

threads.net/thespiritualabode

pinterest.com/thespiritualabode

Printed in Dunstable, United Kingdom